The Right Pathway
to Travel in Life

Miller Allen

TRILOGY
A WHOLLY OWNED SUBSIDIARY OF TBN
PROFESSIONAL PUBLISHING MEETS POWERFUL PROMOTION

The Right Pathway to Travel in Life

Trilogy Christian Publishers

A Wholly Owned Subsidiary of Trinity Broadcasting Network

2442 Michelle Drive, Tustin, CA 92780

Copyright © 2024 by Miller Allen

All rights reserved, including the right to reproduce this book or portions thereof in any form whatsoever.

For information, address Trilogy Christian Publishing

Rights Department, 2442 Michelle Drive, Tustin, CA 92780.

Trilogy Christian Publishing/ TBN and colophon are trademarks of Trinity Broadcasting Network.

For information about special discounts for bulk purchases, please contact Trilogy Christian Publishing.

Trilogy Disclaimer: The views and content expressed in this book are those of the author and may not necessarily reflect the views and doctrine of Trilogy Christian Publishing or the Trinity Broadcasting Network.

10 9 8 7 6 5 4 3 2 1

Library of Congress Cataloging-in-Publication Data is available.

ISBN 979-8-89333-923-9

ISBN (ebook) 979-8-89333-924-6

Dedication

I dedicate this book to my wife, Alice, and to our children, Debra and Donnell, and to their families. To all the Allens and everyone that is connected to our family and to John Sigers, who inspired me to write this book. Special thanks to each editor.

Foreword

My father has a heart for doing what's right. His years of experience have led to these nuggets of wisdom. It is his desire to help and encourage everyone he meets. He also desires to leave tangible jewels to his children, grandchildren and future posterity. You will certainly discover, in these readings, something that will inspire you along this journey of life.

- Debra Allen Pankey

Preface

From the author: As you read this book, I hope you gain inspiration as well as faith, as I have during my young life to my senior life today. If you apply some of these principles to your life, I know, without a shadow of a doubt, you will not fail. Life is an uphill journey, with plenty of challenges in its pathway. They are designed to test you to your very being. Do not worry, for all persons living on this earth, and those who have lived, are facing the same things you are facing, but in a different way. Everyone has a testimony to tell.

In this book, you will find things that will "ring your bell." Don't ignore them; they will let you know which road to take for your success. The good things in this book are yours to grow from. You will also find a lot of wisdom, things proven to make you stronger if implemented and taken to heart. This book will begin with being successful and end with being successful.

Thank you for taking your time to review this book. May God's blessings that I have experienced in my lifetime rest upon you and your family as well.

Miller Allen
February 2016
The Right Pathway to Travel in Life

Table of Contents

Dedication..3

Foreword...4

Preface..5

My Early Life..11

Let's Look at the Butterfly...16

More about My Life..19

What Happens Between Sunrise and Sunset?....................23

Don't Relax Too Long..25

Reflections..26

Success..27

Music - Its Value..28

Our Story..29

Deception and Deceit..31

How to Plan for Your Lifetime Mate..................................32

Things to Do and Not to Do...33

How to Pick Your Friends...34

Who to Partner with..35

Some Things to Never, Never to Do..................................36

How to Appreciate...37

How Did You Get Here?...38

Communicate...39

The Importance of Getting It Right...................................40

What Is Important for Your Children................................41

How to Respond in the Workplace..................................42

What Does the Company Expect from You?..................43

Be Yourself, Don't Fool Yourself...................................45

Why Is Honor Important?...46

Why Is a Relationship with God Most Important?........47

Today Is the Day, My Time Is Now, This Moment........48

A Short Dream..49

Who Truly Are We?..50

Don't Let Anything Stop You..51

Too Late..52

Why I Must Win..53

I Can't Afford to Lose..54

Help with My Situations..55

Pressure..56

I Can, I Will..57

If You Can, I Can Also...58

Surely, I Will..59

Help from the Other Side..60

My Eternal Dream..61

Why the Snake Can't Crawl Straight..............................62

Listening from the Heart...63

What If?..64

Real People Say Real Things..65

Why We All Fail..66

Why Can't I Be Number One?..67

WHILE I LIVE	68
I MUST THINK	69
IN MY LIFETIME	70
MY WIFE	71
GET OUT, STAY OUT	72
FOCUS	73
FROM NONE TO ONE (REAL PURPOSE)	74
SIX FEET DOWNSTAIRS	76
AREA OF CONCERN	78
WHAT SHALL I RENDER TO THIS LIFE?	79
LOOKING IN THE FACE OF REALITY	80
WHAT IS YOUR STORY?	81
POINT TO POINT	82
WHAT ARE YOUR PLANS FOR TODAY?	83
THE MIRROR	84
ATTENTION	85
GENEROSITY	86
SUCCESS	87
CONCLUDING WORDS	88
ABOUT THE AUTHOR	89

My Early Life

The author of this book was born in Winston-Salem, North Carolina on June 4, 1939. He was born to Mary Hunter Ramsey Allen and Mack Slater Allen. Both parents were born in Sumpter, South Carolina, then later moved to Winston-Salem in 1938 to go to work. I was the third child born to this union. I had an older brother, Albert Allen, who was born in Sumpter, SC in 1936 along with an older sister, Barbara Jean, born in 1938, younger sister, Sarah Frances, and a brother, Julius, who passed away in 1984.

My father and mother separated in 1956. My mother went to Detroit, Michigan to live because she had three sisters there. Later, my older and younger brothers and younger sister moved to Detroit. My sister still resides in Detroit. My mother went home to be with God on Sunday, July 5, 2015.

While living in Winston-Salem for all of my life, I recall living in the Boston area of the city at an early age. I also recall riding on a bicycle with a young man we called Bubba Smoot and falling off the bike and hurting my left knee. This experience is the only thing I can remember while living in the Boston section of town. I was about six years of age or younger.

We later moved to East Seventh Street, now New Walkertown Road, in the early 40's. This was during World War II. Lights would go out and warning sounds were heard. To be exact, we lived on Seventh and Dunleith Avenue. We then moved to 714 Locust Avenue, the second house down from Rising Star Baptist Church, where the Rev. Van Landingham was the pastor. We sometimes attended his church when not attending our home church, First Calvary Baptist Church, where Rev. Wilson was pastor. After a stay at First Calvary, we later joined Alpha and Omega Church, which we assisted the Rev. Belva Williams to start in her basement on Gray Avenue. It moved to Dunleith Avenue and then back to Gray Avenue where it is now located.

I remember Rev. Williams and her husband would share food with our family. She was very generous and a very lovely lady. She would use prayer beads; I didn't understand this custom. One song that I still remember was "Let it breathe on me, let it breathe on me, let the Spirit of the Lord, breathe on me." Exposing children to church is a win-win situation in any society. It gives a child a lasting impression. I thank my mother for trying to surround us with a church environment. It has lasting effects. The Church has the power to change a nation. The Church gave us a spiritual outlook on life and taught us the fear of God. The impact of the church is very important in life-building skills that will help a person live a productive life and have skills that will carry one through life, trusting and depending on God for our sufficiency. Church is the only place where one can get the strength to go through the problems in life with the assurance that the God of Gods will be with us throughout our lives. The Church taught us to respect God, but I would not say we were saved. We believed in God, that He existed, but full commitment was not always there. As a young boy, I thought that being a Christian meant you had to give up profanity and many other things that were not good. Our household tried to do the right things, but sometimes we came up short.

When I was 15 years old, I stayed with a family that had just lost two sons in two separate auto accidents. The family was left with only two daughters. I only stayed there six months, and this experience gave me a new outlook on life, for they provided me with many things that my parents could not afford. I really appreciated that family for providing for me and treating me as a son after they had lost their two sons. They made sure that I went to church each Sunday. They also made sure I had proper clothing for school and plenty of food to eat. These things were very good for me!

My family later moved to 7½ Street for a short period of time before moving completely out of this community to Dreamland Park, which was in the northeastern part of Winston-Salem. During my junior year of high school, students in this area were attending Carver High School. I attended Atkins High School, which was one of two high schools located only about four to five miles apart. I had very good teachers, but didn't take full advantage of my education. I did not study and did not like to read. I thought school was very hard and only liked physical education and shop class. My focus was to just get out of school so I could get a job. I knew I would work very hard and master anything that I was going to do. There is a special bond that we form with our schoolmates. You began to appreciate the people you associate with. Both Atkins and Carver were attended by Black students. Carver was mostly a rural school. Atkins had a winning tradition in the state of North Carolina and had the largest enrollment. It was a leading school for sports and academics. Carver was on Carver School Road, which was a very nice community and is still nice today. Carver also had great achievers that are yet doing well in society today. But Atkins won the most games against Carver. Yet, in my senior year, Carver beat us in football. My wife graduated from Carver and I graduated from Atkins. My wife also attended Winston-Salem Teacher's College (now Winston-Salem State University) and received her degree. I was also privileged to attend WSSU for two years.

In order to succeed in life, one should start at the bottom and gradually move up each year. One should set goals and be the best he can be at whatever goal he has set. My mother was my greatest motivator. She taught us to work hard and do a great job. She drilled these things into her children daily. There was no getting around them. We thought she was too hard and overbearing, but as we look back, she was right in preparing us for the long run.

Don't be outdone; reach out there and you can touch it. You can even own it. All things can be accomplished through time, patience, hard work, honesty, perseverance, and integrity. Other guides to success include: don't let failures stop you; don't listen to people that talk down to you and tell you what you cannot do. Just go for it. Additional factors to remember are to take no short cuts and remember that the straight path is always better in the long run. The straight path is the shortest path to reality.

There is power in principles which form true and solid foundations on which to build true success. One should always build with faith in God, knowing that His standards are the true cornerstone, tested and proven in standing firm today, and will stand forever. Don't try to be like anyone else; be yourself. Have core values and stick to them; they will carry you through to be a winner in life.

We should not just talk about it, but be about it. These principles will work for us if we are willing to give them a try. Give them an honest try daily, through thick or thin. Let the test prove us faithful.

The test can be the down payment to get us where we should be. If we pass the test of hardships and disappointments, we can get to the top of our journey without any doubt. Hardships will get us there.

This book is true to my knowledge with its written contents. As the writer of this book, my desire is not to put anyone to shame or blame society for their stay here on this earth. All things happen to us for a reason. I also know that there are two sides to every story or thing. If we can only understand the other side thoroughly, maybe our opinions would differ. In most cases, the other side is not seen or even revealed to us. So, we go on living to be half-opinionated people. Simply, there is a reason why the sun takes water from the earth and the clouds, and brings it back in the form of rain. Simple things, we think, but a great purpose is behind each act. It is very important to know why we all are living today, and we have witnessed many others who are gone forever.

You might ask yourself, "What is my purpose in life?" Are you really sure about your purpose or are you still trying to find a purpose for living? It may be that you and I will have to hurry and find the answers, because we doubtless have less time than we think. It won't be the same with us always, because things are going to change to and with us. This is an example of the process of life's journey.

Let's Look at the Butterfly

A man in New York was looking out of his window when he saw a cocoon. The cocoon gradually cracked open. He saw the wings partly come out and the legs struggling to get out. It looked like the creature was having a hard time coming out, so he decided to help the butterfly over the last hurdle. When he did, the butterfly died. We must follow the life-cycle plan in order to live. The butterfly would not have been seen just months ago, because it was a cocoon. But as time passes, the cocoon develops into a beautiful, colorful, wide-winged butterfly. Time has produced many beautiful things. On vacation, we can be in awe over the beauty of this world. We can find something different and beautiful in each state as we travel on our way. Each state has something in it that is magnificent and beautiful. When traveling to different countries, we see things that we didn't even imagine were in the world.

Life is temporary and we have no assurance that we will see tomorrow. We are always at the mercy of Almighty God. We must walk softly before God each day. We must learn to forgive men of their trespasses, if we want forgiveness. It is safe to say that when we are in trouble, we want forgiveness from others. In life, each day is a learning experience. We must learn from others' mistakes and grow stronger by the things we face in everyday life. We must experience learning to listen, observe and put things into action that will allow us to accomplish much. We must be wise and plan for success every day of our lives.

A simple plan must be followed. Stay on track, and truly success will be yours. Standards are set for successful people only because you have established goals toward which you are working daily. You must not give up, and eventually you will arrive at your goal. You must pay the price of taking the right advice, stay focused, continue moving in the right direction, and follow your heart. Another word of advice is, don't listen to contrary things or persons. Go for it sometimes in secret, but always put God's way and instructions before you. Everyone can achieve success in life according to their God-given ability, one way or another. I become very disgusted when I see people with talents using drugs, wasting away precious beauty that cannot be replaced, making bad choices in marriages, and married persons cheating on each other. Cheating is so unfair, for such a holy vow to be put on the sideline. This brings on hurt in a family that is hard to repair.

Life is so precious, and everything we do will affect someone in some way. So, we must teach ourselves to do the right thing all the time. In most cases, you will have a great outcome. We must always put ourselves in the place of the other person and see if we would like to be treated as we are treating others.

Life is taking inventory of ourselves each day, utilizing each small detail or action. We should not take things for granted. We should seek life's hidden treasures daily. We should anchor our souls in what is true; see with our spirits; guard our hearts from evil; be thankful for hard knocks; and strengthen ourselves in God's grace, for we are not alone. No matter how dark it may seem, we must remember that our shadow moves with us in our dark days. Our shadow is no harm to us, it just reflects our presence.

I have one hand for myself and the other is to help my fellowman, friend or foe. This is how life moves along. Each day our invisible wings are growing and one day we shall fly away. History will tell our story and forget our past. So, you might ask, what is important? The moments we have right now, making the best of them. As long as it affords our stay, we look to and trust in God for everything. In thanksgiving, we humbly bow to the God most holy; the heavens cannot contain Him or His awesome power. He makes the kingdoms of this world to tremble and He alone takes down all authority from all that oppose Him. How sad when we exhaust our temporary frame, just to give it up to the dust from which we have come. If only we can realize our short stay here isn't long enough to be too content. Preparation in this life is very important, for it gets our minds on our eternal destination after our days on earth are finished.

"Lord, always help me to make the right decisions in the time that I have left on this earth, I pray, Amen."

More about My Life

Our childhood was very rocky because my parents had a hard time making ends meet. There was limited income. My father worked for a termite exterminating company, which didn't pay that much. As a result of the chemicals used in the treatments, my father developed cancer of the bone and passed away at the age of 62 in 1974. As a child, I would pick blackberries in the summer and sell blackberry wine for $2 a pint. We saw our share of violence on "The Branch" where our house stood. Many people would get drunk and begin fighting. There were serious breakdowns in our family relationships because there was not 100% unity in our family. That is why I hated alcohol!

We are so privileged to live in this country called America. It was meant to be so from the beginning of creation. It is very interesting to look back and think of the good times as well as the times when things were not so good. Having an older brother and sister and a younger brother and sister puts me in the middle of everything in the family's situation. When I was 16 years of age, my father and older brother were working for me. There was a vacant building on Seventh and Graham Avenues, where Carolina Linen, a garment cleaning business, had moved to another location in the Stratford Road area. A businessman from Durham leased the building to begin refurbishing discarded barrels from R.J. Reynolds Co. We were to take the tin and broken pieces off and refinish the good ones by stacking them in certain piles and numbers. For each pile or number, we were paid a certain price. One week, I was blessed to make almost twice as much as my father was making. I made $60 that week. After seeing my paycheck, my daddy and brother came and worked for me. I witnessed how many of the workers were focused and this got my attention. One man would not eat pork and my interest was piqued because of his great work ethic and discipline. I quit eating pork for about six months because of what he had said. I found out that he was a Muslim. I did not convert to that faith, but was impressed by how he lived and worked. The summers of my junior and senior years, I worked at R.J. Reynolds Tobacco company parttime.

When I was 17, I became serious with God. I had terrible dreams of my teeth scraping the ground behind a car, which was going at a high rate of speed. Also, I saw myself in the house, getting burned up, and I could not get out. These things tormented me, I could not get them out of my mind. At the end of the year, December 1958, a friend of mine, Alvin, came to pick me up to find girls. We went to Cleveland Projects and started speaking with two young ladies in the house when a catastrophe almost happened. Two men knocked on the door. My friend showed me a weapon and said we would get them. I was afraid because I had never been in a fight. When one of the girls opened the screen door, Alvin knew one or both of the men. That is what saved us. I left when the father of the two daughters came to the house, I went out and sat in the car and had time to think about what could have happened if Alvin had not known those men. Conviction came into my heart. I went home and got on my knees and told God if He would help me, I would never go back into the streets again. I heard them shooting to bring in the new year, 1959, but I had a new heart and a new perspective on life. I started a new journey and asked God for strength to help me, and He did. I was able to quit the tobacco factory, because I thought tobacco was hurting people. I got a job at a clothing store on Liberty and Fourth Streets, making $25 a week. After working for about a month, I requested a raise, and was given a $5 raise and worked 10 months for $30 a week. At Christmastime, when the store was crowded, shoes were in the basement where I was. Customers would ask me to help them try on certain shoes. I would accommodate them by selling them shirts also. Sometimes, when women would see me behind the counter, they would go to another part of the store. The lady of the store said that I should be placed on commission, but the owner said if he did that, people would boycott his store and go to other stores. I understood, because this was the order of the time. There were no Black salespersons behind the counter. We could not eat in any established restaurant back in that day. There were separate water fountains and bathrooms as well. So, I understood and accepted the customs of that time.

I went to work for Duke Power Company on July 20, 1959. I was paid $1 an hour for two years as a janitor. I was the first Black to receive a promotion and received two additional promotions. I was promoted to meter reader and paid $1.60 an hour for 10 years. I was later promoted to a non-commission sales position and doing office work. At one point, I was the only man in the satellite office in downtown Winston-Salem, at the Liberty Walk office. Remember, I started with this company doing janitorial work. Finally, I was promoted to the Sales/Marketing Department. I sold appliances for twenty-two years, starting as a non-commission salesperson and moving to a commissioned salesperson. The key to all this success is the prayer room I had at work. I prayed each day at work and God led me to organize a prayer council at Duke Power. In this prayer room, I had a board that I knelt on every day. Upon retiring, I gave this prayer board to a special young man. This young man had a wife and two young boys. One of his sons is playing professional basketball today and is one of the premier point guards in the nation. Prayer works!

I often wondered why I was so blessed. Almighty God showed that His hand was on me by the things I gratefully experienced. I learned early the secret of success. When I was 18 years old in 1958, I decided to give my life to God. I accepted the Lord in my life, but I didn't know how to pray. I didn't know the Bible. My mother would send us off to church, which was two doors from our house, but we didn't understand what was called "getting religion." Going to church was a good custom for us. My mother would dress us up and send us to church on Easter Sunday. Most of the children in the neighborhood would go to church on Easter Sunday wearing their new suits and dresses. That was the day of our lives. This made us proud.

We have read about very influential men and women and their great works in their life experiences. One often wonders how they made the most important decisions between their sunrises and their sunsets. God only knows! I guess the most important question for you and me and the rest of the world is, how are we spending our time between our sunrise and our sunset? I believe if we are wiser, we would want to know if we are doing the right things or we are going in the wrong direction. We were born and programmed to go in the right direction. I believe that the decisions we make each minute of our time here on earth are very important to a lot of people and to our Creator. We are made to perform to our highest degree, with all our talents kicking into high gear in order to make it to our sunset. It has been done by so many others and it can surely be done by people today, if we don't stop at disappointments or temporary setbacks, or care what our society thinks about us. Just tell yourself that you are going to make it.

Surely, we are very important to our culture. We can make a contribution, whether it be large or small, if we only try. A person will be very surprised at what he or she can accomplish between sunrise and sunset. I encourage you to go for it. Give it your God-given best shot. Surely, you can make it, without any shadow of doubt. You can make it with God's help. With God's help, you can do anything.

What Happens Between Sunrise and Sunset?

The first thing one should do is to check the time zone in each country, then analyze the activities of the people in each zone of their country. In America, we have Eastern Standard, Central, Mountain, and Pacific Time zones. The sun always rises in the east and sets in the west. Each time zone has some good things happen. Then we also have some very bad things occur. However, the very bad things often overshadow the good things. Bad things seem to get more media coverage. They receive radio, TV, and newspaper headlines, all have been shown or read all over the world. We are historical figures and it is important to use what happens between our mornings, noons, and nights. Time's end is going to bring a lot of surprises to many of us. When our final sunrise becomes our final sunset, what then? Oh, just to think about this seems like it is not a reality, since things are going so well with us today. But I'm told that every three seconds, someone's sunset has arrived; one day it will be my sunset and yours also.

In this life, we have to make important decisions, to take a stand. This sometimes will go against the status quo or our family, friends, or foes. A stand means taking a one-road journey and not looking back. Don't go back. Look ahead, for the best is in front of you. You must set your goal.

You will find people talking about past experiences and losing time saying "What happened yesterday?" We must remember yesterday cannot be changed; it's history.

We have much to do and to get done ahead of us. The only good thing about the past is to grow from past failures and from things that were less important.

People will truly get in trouble for not thinking of ways to improve all phases of their lives. It's always proper to want to grow in all areas of better points in our lives.

To be honest, we have not arrived yet; we have a way to go. Working on ourselves will make us better persons today than we were yesterday. Only wise persons think this way.

Don't Relax Too Long

The delusion is "I'm okay, I know what I'm doing. I'm smart, I've learned." When we come up with this mentality, we are setting ourselves up for a failure in the future. It's just a matter of time, and it will surely catch up with us. We can learn new things each day that will help us understand things we didn't know and we thought we had the answer to. In life every day, we are tested to see where we are and what we need to do to make it better.

Reflections

In writing this book, there are reflections of my personal thoughts and some of the actions I have taken while living 85 years on the earth. As I look at the success and failures, I'm not satisfied until I achieve all or most of the goals I have set in my lifetime. These goals are centered on the Lord's will for my life only. I want to be all I can be, never try to get over on anyone, and never try to seek short cuts to things of value for my future.

I will strive to be my greatest critic and always desire to want the better things. That will make me a better person each day that is given to me by Almighty God, my Savior and best friend.

I don't want to think evil of anyone, but try to encourage people to look for the best in everything and everybody. I am sorry for the shortcuts I took in life on some occasions. When looking back, they were a disaster to me and I will never repeat them again.

Success

Every living person should want to be successful in his or her lifetime here on the earth. To be successful, one will have to take a good look at what this thing consists of. What will be the cost for me? How do I achieve it? What road must I follow to get to this point? We must ask ourselves many serious questions about the principles of success.

Another important question is, how did others get to this point in their careers to be successful? What steps must I take and what procedures must I follow? The blueprint for success has been already printed by men of old and is available for each one that will follow its guide daily.

True success starts with a relationship with the Lord of all Lords and proceeds from there by being faithful to the cause of Christ daily. Without these guidelines, partial success will only go so far. There is a God that is in control of all our success, and He is ready to help us in our failures. We will be successful daily if we ask of Him in faith.

Music – Its Value

The soprano – the voice, the lyric, the word and the sound - breathtaking. Music is a breakthrough that inspires the heart and touches the seat of one's soul.

Yes, it's real soul music. Why is music so powerful? Just a few things about music:

1) It is inspiring
2) Good music rules the soul
3) It brings gladness from sadness
4) It reaches the throne of God; praise music is music for real!

When you sing, sing to inspire, to encourage. Sing to tell your story. Each person on this earth has his or her story to tell. And sometimes, music will let you know who you love and who you are in love with. Listen to good music. There is nothing like it. Its words even touch the lowest of mankind.

Music is so powerful it brings tears to the high and mighty, who are sometimes hard to reach. It is good to write a song or sing a song, but most important, be a song that others will be blessed by the tune of your living daily. Your life is that great soprano; sing it well, someone is listening!

Our Story

Each and every dweller on this earth is given a story. Even your life is a story to someone. My question today is simple, what is your story? Have you ever thought about it? Some of the answers are not hard things to think about. Just simple things you are about throughout your life. In other words, your story is more important than you can and will think. Your story reaches far and wide. It can inspire multitudes, and maybe change a life. On another word of thought, the angels are recording the good deeds you are doing. We think each day of evil or good, and sometimes evil has more power over us by the way we think if we don't bring our minds into the room of God's Word.

Our story should be to ask for help each day, to get things done according to reality and by letting our story be surrounded by the only source of divine help in the word of eternal salvation.

Our story is weak, without divine strength. God is everything that is true and faithful. Ask daily for His help in telling (living) your story.

Going To Heaven Is Like...

A person that is traveling the one-way street of life cannot go backward because the road behind each step he makes closes the path. The only way he can go is forward, up a mountain in order to get to the other side.

He has a cross on his back and the cross is getting heavy climbing up the mountain, so he decides to make his cross lighter by cutting off 12 inches.

He now is not having a hard time climbing his mountain. All of a sudden, he can see his destination on the other side. Now all the toil and hard work seems to come to an end, because just across this hill to the other side, he sees his destination.

But wait a minute. He found that he needed just 12 inches to get to the other side, the same 12 inches that made his cross lighter. Sad to say, he couldn't get across because of the 12 inches he cut off.

This story is a metaphor to show that the cross is designed to get us to heaven. We will not make it if we alter the cross. If we alter the cross, it will be our way and not His way.

Getting to Heaven is like not taking shortcuts to lighten your cross. Ask God for the strength to climb your mountain, in order to get to the other side. If any man would come after Jesus, he will have to take up his cross daily and follow Jesus! This is what Heaven is about, no shortcuts but a one-way journey through this earth.

Deception and Deceit

The opposite of goodness is a thing called deception, which is the evil that tries to fool one into negative behavior. It's been around throughout the ages and we saw it in the Garden of Eden, before you and I got here. The person that was the author is very evil and he will try anything possible to get us to buy into his programs. They will look very enticing and pleasant to the eye, but behind their schemes are hidden motives that are deadly if partaken of.

Deceit is its first cousin, who is telling Deception how to get to a person through many ungodly channels. Deceit is tricky and sometimes hard to recognize, but must be avoided at all times. Deceit shows up almost everywhere to the person that would buy into its program for a very cheap price. But its deception is far too much for the person that buys into it.

How to get around Deceit and Deception?

First thing to do is to check its contents out with Reality. See what it has done for the person that brought its products. Ask them how they are living with these two fellows. If theywill tell you the truth, you will find out that their father is not your father. You would stay away from them as far as the east is from the west.

How to Plan for Your Lifetime Mate

First, get a true relationship with the God of Heaven. Next, ask God whether the person you are pursuing is the right one for you. Ask this person a lot of questions about important facts of life. Don't live together before marriage. Never talk to another person while you are in a relationship with the person you are pursing. Spend time in prayer for this person. Watch for danger signs in your relationship. These things are very important, because when you sign the final papers, it's too late. The ring seals the marriage.

Plan to be the best you can be in your marriage. Plan never to cheat in your marriage, keep it real. Never take each other for granted. Work daily on your marriage. It's what you will make of it. Be faithful through thick and thin.

Truly, the tests will come over and over again. Don't give in. Don't give up. Stay the course. You can make it to the end. If others have stood the test, you can also. Don't give up! Time is counting on you to endure hardships as a good family. Your lifetime partner can become your best friend.

Things to Do and Not to Do

Do set your mind and heart on the Savior of mankind.
Do not deny the Word of God.

Do worship as often as you can.
Do not take worship for granted.

Do take notes on important things.
Do not take warning signs lightly.

Do honor all mankind.
Do not speak ill of anyone.

Do pay your vows.
Do not tell people things just to get them away from you.

Do plan in advance for your family.
Do not put others before your household.

Do respect your minister and his family.
Do not try to condemn your minister.

Do realize you are not perfect.
Do not look for others to be perfect.

How to Pick Your Friends

Bang Bang, Boo Boo, who are you?

Guess what? You are who you associate with. They will make you or break you. No getting around them. Their ways will someday override your ways.

Your friends should be very strong, Christian-minded people, with a goal to please God and God alone.

A true friend, one that can be trusted through good and not so good times, one who will want what is good for you, is hard to find.

A true friend will not betray you, but will back you up and seek your good at all times.

A true friend is a person without any variation, who will warn you of any hidden dangers, ones that they have heard are coming your way.

To pick your friends, you will have to study everyone that seeks to get close to you.

Who to Partner With

Looking down life's super highway, who do I see?
My high school buddy, my first cousin, my running sidekick.
But the question is still in my mind, who shall I partner with?
Well, I think it's time to get serious about my life. When I take a survey, I can see some successful guys.

I think they set the right example for a person to partner with. Their plan is going into the right direction for diversity in a market-driven world of economics.

A person's track record will determine who his partners should be.

Partnering with the best will not make you the less. It's only the true test of your getting through life for total success.

Some Things to Never, Never Do

Never, neverunderestimate anyone,
Never take things for granted.

Never cheat in your marriage,
Never give judgment toward a person.

Never say no when you know the answer is yes.
Never put anyone on the spot to embarrass them.

Never do less that your best.
Never forsake worship.

Never take your health lightly.
Never cross train tracks when the light is flashing.

Never put off today for tomorrow
Never say the Bible is wrong.

Never take God's Word lightly.
Never think that you have it all together.

Never say everybody sins; I can get away with it if I sin, then repent when I'm finished.

How to Appreciate

Generosity is important. It doesn't cost much to be courteous. It's worth very much in respecting those who receive it from you.

To appreciate a thing is proper, to let someone know you are pleased with what they have done as a favor to you.

Appreciation is giving to another person, in some kind of way, what someone else has given to you.

How should we appreciate our being on this earth?
One way is to worship the God that made this life happen for us.

For it is He that has made possible our moving and having our being even now.

To say, "Thank You, Lord" would not be out of order or to praise God each day would not mean that you are out of order.

God likes it when we pass to others some of the things He has given unto us.

How Did You Get Here?

Before our parents were born, God knew that we would be here. In God's providence, we were thought of: how wonderful that is.

That's why we should think about what we can do to let Him know that we thank Him for smiling on us.

We got here by the mercy of Almighty God, and God made us in His image, to reflect His love to His people---from our hearts to theirs.

Our parents were only the vehicles, but the Lord was the life in the vehicle, to make sure we would not drown in the flood, but make it safely into His hands.

We must not forget that the Almighty God, our heavenly Father, had everything to do with our coming into this life safely on this earth.

All our steps were ordered by the Lord, for it is He that is in total charge of all things.

We got here by God's mercy and His amazing grace. Thanks be to our God.

Communicate

If only we could communicate, there would be many more people living today.

Not communicating has and is depriving families, friends, nations, races, creeds, and many others. It has kept a lot of people from being in step with one another.

Why? What is the reason people don't trust each other? I believe the list would be too long to put in any book or manuscript. You would hear some silly things as well as major issues. Sometimes, communication can clean up a lot of misconceptions. If people could see the motive behind the actions, a lot of things would be clear in their thoughts. As we want to communicate with God through prayer, we also should seek to communicate with all mankind, knowing this is the only way to break through the fog and misconceptions of each other.

The Importance of Getting It Right

There is no substitute for the right way.
It belongs in the field of the highest standard in the world.
Right-thinking people always want to get it right, for they know that iron sharpens iron.
Hanging out with persons who are trying to keep it right is powerful, for they are living on the wings of a divine power, and that is awesome.
Getting things right in life makes you a target. You will at times be tested by those that are contrary, and they will try to break into your heart with deception, hiding behind a smiling face, or charming ways to entice you to forget your standards, and come down and enjoy yourself with the world.
To you and me, we have but one time to get it right. It is very important that we do just that and keep it right every day we are privileged to live on God's earth.
Keeping this life's journey right is the most precious thing to do.

What Is Important for Your Children

The things that are important for my children today are to keep them motivated and focused on what will make them strong in order to make a good showing in this life that is ahead of them.

Our children need to see our lives as a reflection of what Christ was about when He was in this world.

It is important that we set a good example of righteousness as a guide for their success.

God and God alone can make this possible, if only we listen to Him through His Word.

The words we say around our children are words they will process when they are not around us. We are very important to our children. We are held accountable for how we raise our precious little ones.

What is important for our children is they are growing faster than we can imagine. We have to let them know that God is with them as long as they are with Him.

How to Respond in the Workplace

It's just a blessing in this day and time to have a job. Having a job is just the beginning of it. How to keep the job is the other important part.

There will be many challenges on the job. You will have to prepare yourself.

Please do not think that you have it made at all. You will have to prove to the company that you are the one that truly fits in.

By your performance, you will be judged daily. You will have to be at your very best and always know that what you do will determine your future on the job.

Sometimes, you will have to out-perform the next person for you to have a future in the company.

One thing never to do is form a relationship with a person that you admire or the person that will try to entice you.

Keep everything business! Be serious in your employment. Remember, that is what you were hired to do. Do it well; doing it right means a bright future just may come your way.

What Does the Company Expect from You?

The company wants you to represent their logo with your best intentions. For you are the company; you make the company honorable by the manner in which you conduct yourself at work or wherever you are. People identify you as an important person in the community for the job you have been doing for your company. Remember to always be aware that you are important to your job.

What the company did for me-

I can truly say, I was blessed by working at Duke Power. I received a lot of support from the employees. We connected very well. When people know each other by working together, it will open up understanding in race relations. I have found that the more we work together, the more we do understand each other, that we have the same things in common.

The company gave me three promotions, gave me an opportunity to serve on the Safety Committee, worked with Junior Achievers, and when I retired, I was given a chance to become president of the retirees for two years and later serve on the Board of Retirees. I also was given a chance to sit on the Board for one day in Charlotte when promoted to marketing.

My wife and I were blessed to receive five free trips, three to the Bahamas, one to Disney World and one to New York. I was proud to have worked for then Duke Power (now Duke Energy), 1959-1993. To God be the glory for the things He did for me.

Although I couldn't sell at the clothing store, by being patient and faithful to Almighty God, He made a way for me to work adjacent

to the same building on Liberty Street and sit behind a desk and sell appliances for a multimillion-dollar company. Faith in God pays off. Dedication, hard work, and Godliness will take anyone to the top.

From none to one--what a story.

Be Yourself, Don't Fool Yourself

Everyone should take inventory of oneself. See your strong points as well as your weak points.

Do not try to be like the next person. You were made to perform with the ability that God has given you.

Fooling yourself is like saying it's raining when the sun is shining. It also is like putting salt in your coffee instead of sugar.

Be yourself. Don't try to gain the respect of people by enlarging your innertube, because very soon the air is going to seep out of it.

Fooling yourself is also creating yourself out of the true values in this life.

Sooner or later, time will show everyone the true you. What you plan will one day come up in this life. All will know whether you were true or false.

Be all that God has made you to be and you will surprise yourself.

Why Is Honor Important?

In school, in life, in general, everyone likes to be recognized.

High achievement is good for each and every one. The world glorifies its high achievers.

The newspapers sell more papers when the names of high achievers appear in their paper or in books.

There is great market for high achievers, and the job market is looking for high achievers.

Honor is important in that it is a step above. The person who is honored has achieved milestones that others never may get to achieve in their lifetime.

Honor means someone has spent time and energy to get to the highest level in life possible.

Honor brings respect, produces character, gives recognition, promotes greatness and sets a person with the elite people one the earth.

Why Is a Relationship with God Most Important?

Could you measure time? Do you know when you are going to leave this earth—the date, the final seconds, what the weather will be, what the temperature will be? Do you know how many people will come to your funeral and the names of those attending?

Well, let's go back a little farther. What was the day and hour you knew you would be born? I think I better ask you some things more in your thinking realm.

Count the hairs on your head. Count the grains of sand on the earth. Measure all the water in the oceans and seas. Count each tree that is in the world, and when you are through, go a little higher and tell me how many clouds are in the sky. I know you are smart; just look up and start counting.

Well, we are not through yet. I would like for you to get out your scales and measure all the air that we are breathing. Tell me how many fish are in the seas and oceans.

Our relationship with the God that made these things and knows the answers to all these things is very important, because He made all these things for us to enjoy and not try to know more than Him.

Today Is the Day, My Time Is Now, This Moment

The saying is "time and tide wait for no one." It is also said that "tomorrow is promised to no one."

The time we have at this moment is very precious to us, because someone, somewhere, just ran out of time.

Your time, my time, this moment, we should cherish. It's very important. We can't imagine what will happen if we lose these important moments.

Everything happens in its day, moment, and time. Our time is right now. This means I must get to work and get things done now, or very soon, or things will pass me by.

If only I would stop putting things off until a later day. Sometimes, and more times than we think, we put off too much, and some things never get done.

Today is the day. Let's get started. Each day will bring us closer and closer to reality.

The time is right now. The moment is when you get in gear and get your motor running by putting your actions in the right gear.

A Short Dream

Life is but a short dream. When we wake up, it's all over. After this life is real living in Hell or in Heaven. Our choices are made by our daily lifestyles.

We all will have to answer to the One that brought us into His world and give account for our stewardship here. It is important never to take this life for granted. We don't have the method or power to keep ourselves here, for there is a time that we all must give an eternal goodbye to this earthly life. What then?

Who Truly Are We?

Soul, body, flesh & spirit.

Dust from the earth. Dark dust, light dust, brown dust, red dust, and dust that is between these colors. Behind the dust, we are all alike, from one set of parents.

We all eat alike, we all hurt alike, we all drink water, and will all die one day. No one has a monopoly on life. We cannot buy one day with a trillion dollars. We cannot prolong our lives here on the earth.

Our souls tell us there is a higher power. The soul has a passion in the end to be in His presence.

Our bodies are fearfully and wonderfully made, in the image of Almighty God.

Flesh is what we are; spirit dwells inside of our fleshly bodies.

The spirit is the thing that puts us in motion to discern good and evil, and empowers us to overcome the evil that surrounds us daily.

Who we are, or what we do, comes from the things we put into our hearts.

The issues of all activity from u, originates from our hearts.

We are the words we speak daily, and the things we do at all times.

Don't Let Anything Stop You

First, you must speak to yourself and say without a shadow of doubt, "I am going to make it in this life. I'll let nothing stop me, for if some people are successful, I can be also."

Success starts with the right relationship; we must have a real foundation of faith, found only in our Creator. Daily listen to His voice as He speaks to us through His scriptures that will keep us on a path proven to make us more than conquerors.

I'm not telling you what I think, I'm telling you what I know. For in my lifetime, I have seen this principle work over and over in several persons, including my life.

Too Late

Too late, it's all over; when life ends, what then?

What sad words. Too late means I just missed it. I have no more chances. What is the next step?

It's all over; my end has come. It's all over; my entire life is now in the past.

All humankind will one day get to this very point in time; what then?

When life ends, we will be with God eternally or in hell forever.

The choice was made by us and by us alone. What we have done in this life will determine our future, one way or the other.

What will happen then will depend on whether we accepted and trusted in an Almighty God or we lived to please people and ourselves.

It is very sad to hear the words, "too late." Also, the words, "it's all over." Life had ended.

The way to make sure you are secured when you leave here is to have an honest relationship with God by receiving Jesus Christ as Lord and Savior, and keeping His Word daily, trusting what He says through the Scriptures.

Why I Must Win

If we all try hard enough, we too can win. Winning is giving it all we have and not looking back.

Winners never quit and quitters never win. My goal is trying and trying and trying each day to get there.

Maybe one day I will get there, if I don't give up.

Hope keeps us in the race. Someone will win, why not me?

If we don't give in or give up, we will win anything we attempt to do.

The test is my endurance, my patience, my desire.

Losing is for the other person, not me.

The formula for winning is very simple. Always acknowledge God our Father, and ask Him His direction for my life.

I must win because I have built in me a great desire to get anything that will bring glory to our God. I thank Him for letting me win and empowering me to win.

I Can't Afford to Lose

Losing is wasting your precious time. I can't lose because it would cost me too much. Why lose when you can be a winner; doesn't it make sense?

Losing is too risky for anyone, because when you lose, someone will notice it.

No team enjoys losing a game.

It breaks down morale, it weakens the will, and sometimes weakens the mind.

We can't afford to lose because gaining is more important.

We can win if we stick to our game plan by putting the best player into our game.

We can't lose with the Holy Spirit, with Jesus, and with Almighty God on our side.

With all this power and authority on our side, we cannot afford to lose.

Help with My Situations

Some things will come that we cannot control, no matter how we think we have a handle on them.

Our situations are different but the same stress comes in life matters, something hard to figure out.

My mind is good and capable of being on top of a lot of things, but sometimes our pain is out of control.

Situations are common for all mankind. But getting the proper help is hard to come by.

First, you have to have trust in someone to share your struggles with.

Second, you must be honest and face your situation as soon as possible. Say to yourself that enough is enough. I'm going to beat this thing that is before me.

Third, you must have the confidence in knowing that others have gotten over the same thing you are now facing; there is nothing new under the sun.

There is help in all the things we will face in our lifetime, if only we can find the right source for our situation.

Pressure

Sometimes, pressure is good and sometimes it's not so good, but pressure is necessary.

Pressure proves how strong a thing is, or how strong a person is.

Pressure is the true test of endurance. It will prove the product, and if it passes the pressure, it will be marketable.

Pressure separates the weak from the strong. Pressure makes or breaks you or whatever it is applied to.

To a human, pressure can make one confess or be terrified and lie, just to be relieved.

We will all face pressure in many different ways. When we are not aware of it coming our way, it will come all of a sudden, and the results will be good or not so good.

When pressure comes to you, just think of these few lines and say to yourself, "I heard this before."

To win the battle when pressure comes is to be empowered with the Holy Spirit and follow His direction.

I Can, I Will

I can be successful, and I will, for I will be caught trying each day.

I can overcome negative things that are coming my way. I can do this by thinking positively when those things come my way.

To do the positive, I must tell myself I have the same opportunity that the next person has.

If I try and try hard enough, I'll get there. I will give it my best shot in order to attain my goals.

Hard work will get me the great rewards that are in front of me.

I can do all things through Christ who strengthens me.

I can only do this through the one who has all the power in this life, who can empower me to do the things that are honest and fair in my lifetime.

I can, if it's the Lord's will, win the battles in this life that are facing each and every one that dwells on this earth.

If You Can, I Can Also

If you can get to the top of your mountain, you can climb higher than you are today, one step at a time will make it happen.

The starting point is today, right now.

I have seen how others have had so much doing it the right way and getting it to their next level, why not me?

What is your plan of action? It must have been carefully sought out, planned and researched very well, and now the results are well worth the start.

I can also achieve by looking in the right direction and staying the course, trusting in the God of Gods, and the Lord of Lords; what a mighty plan to have these great persons from the foundation of heaven to be our companions here with us, as we dwell on His earth.

Trying with all I have been given in knowledge and wisdom and faith in God, I will also be successful, for if you can ,I can also.

Surely, I Will

    I will seek for things that will help me to be better in all the things that are very important in my lifetime, things that would be the best interest for me and the persons I come in contact with.

    Surely, I will seek for all good that have been given to me to make it through this life in a positive way. I will also look daily for ways to improve my status in the things that are true and real.

    I will surely be zealous of important things that have proven to be winners for the masses,

    things that count the most, when it comes to productivity in producing the best possible outcome.

    If it can be done, surely, I will give it a try.

    First step – examine myself to see where I stand in life.

2) Do what it takes to correct any problems I come upon.

3) I will trust in the Lord to get the proper guidance for the day.

Help from the Other Side

There will come a time in this life when we will need help from the other side.

The side of the ones that are stronger than we are, in many things that life brings your way.

These things come to all mankind, for us to get prepared for a lot of things that are not present today, but will pop up in our near future.

Preparation is the key to obraining what we need to get through many situations.

Sometimes the other side is more equipped to get all the help we are in need of.

And pride will sometimes tell us, we can handle it all by ourselves.

If you really want the answer to your problems, you may have to get your help from the other side.

Make sure the other side is biblically sound.

My Eternal Dream

Many people dream of great things, like a good job, fine house, big car or riches, etc.

But few think on life hereafter, their eternal dream where things are really beyond our imagination.

Let's face it, we are all going to leave here and we will spend eternity someplace.

Why not dream of a place of peace and tranquility? It is possible to be at this place when our earthly life has ended.

What will it take to inherit my eternal dream, for this dream to come true?

What I think may not be the best answer, but what does God say about this question?

To dream is good, to implement the dream by having an obedient spirit is the answer to the dream.

To get to eternity in the right place, we have to think about the God of eternity and follow His ways today.

Why the Snake Can't Crawl Straight

The snake was one called the serpent. He has many names that no one would like to be identified with.

His ways are all ways of manipulation and very poisonous to human society.

He cannot crawl straight because of his nature, and everyone who follows him cannot be straight.

There are snakes who crawl sideways and the others are crooked crawlers.

The snake was seen in the Garden of Eden, and the results of listening to him were disastrous.

The snake was also seen in Matthew and Luke, trying to get Jesus to take his bait and lose his position in God's will, but each time the devil came, Jesus was ready to defend the truth.

The devil is crawling at mankind every day, trying to get his program established in them through his cunning ways.

If you are not straight up with everybody, watch out! You may have given in to this crooked fellow.

It's good to walk straight always.

Listening from the Heart

Listening sometimes is hard to do, for we say we hear, but do we really? That is another thing.

But listening to one's heart is a great factor in implementing and processing information that has been heard.

You can tell the people that are listening from their hearts. They are the ones you can somehow trust, because their lives reflect their actions coming from their hearts.

These actions are positive and Godly in nature.

These are the people that get a lot done for others; they do productive things that always make a difference.

To listen from the heart is productive in that it is the very thing that makes a person a true follower of the right things society has in common.

Listening from the heart brings a person into the best of the best for true success in the strategies of making the best decisions in this life day by day.

What If?

What if heaven is real? Don't you think each person should try to get there?

What if I die and miss heaven; what do you think would happen to me?

What if the Bible is right and I am wrong, what then?

What if the sun stops shining, and the clouds don't bring rain to the earth, what do you think would happen next?

What if all religions were wrong except Christianity? What do you think would happen when the end of civilization comes?

What if your beliefs are wrong when it comes to your interpretations, what then?

What if you die before you repent of your sins and you do not get things right with your fellowman, what then?

What if you believe God's Word daily for your living on this earth? What then can you expect the answer of your commitment to bring you?

Real People Say Real Things

There is no substitute for the real thing, and it is always good to be around people who you know are saying real things.

These people know that to keep it real is a product of God's Word, for the Word of God is real and true from the beginning; nothing false can be found in God's Word.

For people to be real means a person would have to take on the nature of God, by becoming one of His followers.

To say real things is not easy for everyone. There are consequences for speaking the truth in this world.

People will distance themselves from you when you do not agree with their system of understanding.

You have to process most everything you hear in order to get to the bottom of things that are told you.

Sometimes just one thing will counter all other things said, because that one thing is not the truth.

Real people will always say real things because they will be speaking what's in their hearts.

Why We All Fail

I would like to think that at times I am a failure, but this is not the case with me.

Sometimes, I think I have a certain thing right, but when I weigh it with reality, it comes up short.

Sometimes we fail because we do not understand a thing, sometimes we fail because we think we know and no one can tell us it is different.

Most of the times we fail for lack of knowledge. In order not to fail so much, we must learn as much as we can and put our knowledge into everyday obedience to what we have learned.

Some people fail because they are lazy. They know, but they don't care about doing what they know is right.

Failure is not a good friend for us to associate with, for it brings disaster to the masses each day and embarrassment to a lot of persons.

The chief thing of our failures is that we are not willing to let our Father lead us by the hand of our mind through this wilderness called life.

Why Can't I Be Number One?

There are many people seeking to be the best in whatever things they are in, and that's good.

There are many benefits in being the number one person in your business, company, church, or family; that person stands out in everything they are involved in.

This person isn't hard to recognize, because they seem to work a little harder than the next person, they seem to be committed to a cause, to doing things by the book as closely as possible.

And they are committed to faith in a power that empowers them to succeed.

Why I can't be number one? Maybe I don't put forth the effort. Maybe I'm not willing to pay the price it's worth.

Believe me, there are reasons we can come up with to tell ourselves we can't be number one.

1) We don't think that we are qualified.
2) We think others have more potential than we have.
3) We fail because we stop trying.

Why can't I be number one? It is because I'm too lazy to use all my God-given talents to strive for it.

While I Live

While I live, the answer isn't hard to figure out. Why I live is a gift from God for me to love Him for His gratitude to me.

I should pass blessings to others, as blessings have been given to me. I did not have to buy these things God has given to me, things I could never afford.

While I live, I know that life is not living unless you figure out your purpose for being here.

While I live, I will see to it that I pass my blessings to those I meet, that are in need of life's necessities.

Why I live is the Lord's will for me to be on His earth for the purpose of enjoying His blessings and passing the torch to others.

To live on the earth is a blessing from God, to make this world a better place, to influence someone for something that is positive.

I live to be a testimony that God and God alone is to be praised for all I have, and all that comes my way on His earth.

I Must Think

Thinking is a gift, to go in the right direction, to think is to be wise to make great and wise decisions.

In order to overcome the negative, we must think about how much greater the positive is.

Before we accomplish anything worthwhile, we must think about the work we have to put into the efforts it will take to finish the task.

I also must think before I make any decisions to do anything and everything that I am able to do.

I must also think about others and what they are experiencing, in order to get through this life.

Even before marriage, I must consider all the pros and cons about what I am going to get into.

Planning is a great part of thinking about where I'm going in this life, and how shall I get things in order to accomplish the things necessary to make things work in an orderly way?

I must think about my end as well as my being here now at this time in history.

In My Lifetime

I have all the tools in front of me to push forward, if only I use them properly.

There is no complaint that I can't do this or any thing. All I need I have, if only I can stop complaining and get busy and go to work. All I have to do is to look forward and march to the tune of implementation.

Forward is the only way toward positive solutions. This road leads to greater and greater things that everyone desires to accomplish in life.

But, if we use our gifts to go forward in an honest way, we will be proud of the time that was used to get our goals met.

I must not covet others but use all the tools in my space each day possible.

Sitting down, dreaming overtime, won't get it done. Complaining is the disease that defeats all good desires to get the job done.

To build your project properly, you need to go all the way toward the thing you desire.

God has given to you and me the right tools for the right project, that you and I have to face in our lifetimes.

My Wife

My wife is half of my life, close to me as my side is to me.

I must take her with me at all times, that is liking what she likes, and hating what she doesn't like.

Having my wife's desires for me is very important. My wife is to be respected at all times, in every place, with or without her presence with me!

I must never go against her wishes at any time. She is to be respected whether absent or present.

My wife is very important because she shares my house and everything I have.

There will be no secrets between the two of us, for to be honest is the only way to have a great marriage.

My wife is my best friend; only God's love is better. Through life, in sickness or anything that comes our way, I must, without any doubt, take good care of my wife at all times, no substitutes.

Thank God for a good wife, supportive, faithful to the end, a Proverbs 31 wife.

Get Out, Stay Out

Time and time again, going behind those bars, hearing steel touching steel with a loud noise. There's nothing like it, to send a message that you are in a cage, and that's not how it should have been for you in this life.

Cages are for animals. Men have the ability to take charge in life, but when you are in jail, the jail is in charge of you and the rules have to be enforced, or else!

I'm told, when the lights are out, men cry. Their wills are broken down; where is their dignity? All rules are set for them with no exceptions.

If we don't take earnest heed in life, hard times will surely be our reward, and we bring it on ourselves.

There have been some good lessons learned in jail. Sometimes, it was the right place for a lot of persons. You can hear things like, "If it hadn't been for me being here, I may have lost my life." "Now that I see what real life is about, I am changing my behavior and turning in the right direction, and getting back on the right track."

There have been so many success stories coming from life behind bars. All persons should hurry and find themselves, for we have but one time in this life on earth and we will be out of here.

The proper thing to do is get out, stay out, and live to be productive in this society.

Focus

Don't let your mind set on your behind, because you will always be down, where you don't belong.

Since this life affords each of us one opportunity, we must take the time to think about which way we must go to make our lives a success story.

As we look back in time, we can see how many have passed this way and are not with us anymore; their work is finished. Their opportunity is over.

Ready or not, their record is recorded of the good and the not so good things that they accomplished while here.

My plan is to seize the moments that I have left on the earth and do the things that I have been designed to do with all that is within me.

Thinking in these terms, I feel obligated to think about my divine assignment almost daily. What can I do with the time given to me today, and each day I am here on God's earth? How am I spending each day in preparation toward this important cause?

Some important questions come to my mind daily. What are you doing to make a difference in this world?

I know that is the reason I am here, and been given the ability to think this way. So, I struggle with this, I deal with this daily in my mind.

From None to One (Real Purpose)

In life, there is purpose. Purpose will require planning and planning requires thinking in the right direction toward the positive. To get to the positive features, there will be many setbacks in which patience will be the by-product to help you achieve your goal. What goals have you set?

Having the right mind is to get with people who are like-minded as you and will be important toward your goal.

There are no short cuts in achieving your success. You will have some disappointments, but it is only temporary, just to see if you are serious about where you are going. The bottom line is not to stop when discouragement comes. It is coming many times, over and over. To get to precious metal, important things require hard work. Never count yourself out. Just try a little harder when things come to a standstill.

Any and all successful persons had to go through a valley of disappointments, and so would we.

It's only a test, to test our endurance. Strive a little harder each and every day. If we can take the challenge and stick it out, that's when we accomplish our goal.

Research is an important factor in preparing to get there. Watching others in your same profession will help to steer around some pitfalls. Discerning the times is also a key factor in staying your course.

People who will be successful will be like the stock market's ups and downs. It's only a way of life. We must take the risk.

Don't let this set you back. You have a long road ahead of you, if you stay the course. Like time is changing every day, people are no different. They will say one thing today and reverse it today or tomorrow. You will not go wrong if you count on only one person to lead you in all directions and guide you in all ways. That is God Almighty.

I believe everyone wants to be successful in life, but I believe that only a few really try. Being successful is following a proven script.

Six Feet Downstairs

In the cemetery, there are brilliant minds that did not develop, franchises that never made the books, and books that were never written. We will never know the things that went undone that would have made a difference in someone's life that were taken to the grave.

One question you and I should ask daily is, "What is my job description in this one and only life I have on the earth?" This question is global, for all creation of mankind.

Only you and I will have to answer this question while we live, because it's too late when we are out of here. Our consciences will not let us rest until we answer this very important question, today.

It will determine our destiny, and what then?

Life is short, and planning for the next step will be our eternal future, whether good or eternal evil.

Each day, we must find ourselves. Sometimes we are wandering too far in the wilderness of life, going places and gaining no ground, wasting life away. We must examine ourselves daily and take inventory and see how we stack up with reality.

Only you can do this for yourself, and there is no substitute. All of us, one day, will give an account for being on this earth, for good or for evil. Time for all of us to get a spiritual check-up. If things are not right, then we must get things fixed before our end comes.

We never know when our day will come to an end, but for sure, our date has already been set.

As the rain waters the earth, good deeds and kindness, gratitude toward the poor, helps water someone's life.

You have, in this short time, experienced your life going from none to number one. Having said this, how happy are you? Congratulations for your patience through your hard work and for not giving up. You are almost there, keep going forward.

Area of Concern

My main area of concern is, what has God required of me? Am I faithful in this area? What can I do to show that I am on target to fulfilling my destiny? These questions stay with me and I am conscious of them daily.

One thing comes up over and over in my mind, the Gospel on Wheels Outreach, a ministry that came to me over a decade ago. The question in my mind is why did I stop pursuing this ministry?

Not working hard enough in the pursuit of this ministry has caused me to be out of focus. For I have seen many things this ministry is about be realized in other ministries and organizations.

So, as I come this day, I pray that the greatest God of us all will grant me the wisdom and knowledge to go forward in getting the proper components for the success of this ministry.

If God is my help, I'll put my whole heart towards carrying out the objectives of this great cause, of helping God's people in this earth. Servant Miller

What Shall I Render to This Life?

This question is a lifetime question that demands answers for each person that dwells upon this earth. I'm told that we are leaving this earth every three seconds, each day. I know that my time is coming some day in the future. The question becomes very important to me; I'm faced with it daily.

Also, I am aware that all creation has its part to play in this life. But important is the question, what decision will I make to show that I am focused on doing good things and not the things that are hurting someone?

Life today and always should be helping fallen humanity up to their feet. When we were down, someone helped us, whether it was human or divine.

Each person is a great part of a puzzle that, when put in place, will make something that is broken or incomplete restored to its full design.

What each one of us does with our piece of this great puzzle is essential to our fulfilling life's journey.

Making the best of each day will make life worthwhile. We must work hard to make this happen.

Life, and real living, is also looking out for your fellowman and putting the other person in your shoes.

Then, maybe you can understand why people act the way they do.

Looking in the Face of Reality

When I look in the face of what is real, what am I looking to see and what do I find? To answer this question, I must first look at myself and wonder how God is seeing me on a daily basis.

Questions come often. What am I doing toward the Lord's will for my life? Am I doing the things that God is requiring of me? What is my relationship when it comes to God's Word? What parts am I doing? What parts do I neglect? Questions come often, running through my mind. I am trying to see where I should be when it comes to the face of reality in this world.

How do I perceive the news events happening daily in this world? What is my judgment of things that are happening in the world today? What stand do I take? Am I in agreement with things that are true and faithful, or do I go with the status quo? Do I try to please people to get their approval of me or do I try to see what is right in God's sight first?

Do I try to obey what I read in the holy writ or do I say that we are not all perfect? How do or will I feel when my life is over? Will I feel that in life I took too many shortcuts in order to get through? Will I feel that I tried with all my heart to do God's will?

In the face of daily actions, these questions will continue to come up and we will have to face reality.

No getting around it.

What Is Your Story?

Behind each and every mind, there could be found a story.

So, my question today is, '"What is your story?" Think about it.

Some of the answers to your story may be your daily life, such as what you do and what you do not do, or where you've been and the things you have experienced.

In other words, your story is very important to more than yourself. You affect your surroundings in one way or another.

If God would reveal your story publicly, I wonder would you feel embarrassed or would you feel happy about what He would say about you?

The angels are recording "our stories on a daily basis. I'm wondering what they are saying about you and me.

When I think of this question, I can only say, "Lord, have mercy on me, and let me always do those things that are pleasing to You daily."

We think each and every day of either good or bad things. Evil sometimes pops its ugly head up, but our prayer is and will continue to be, God have mercy on me.

Help me to focus daily on Your will for my life. Help me to live out the true meaning of salvation through the precious blood of Christ Jesus our Lord and Savior!

Point to Point

How do you know for sure you are going to get from point A to point B?

To get from point A, which is your starting point, to point B, which is your ending point, you must have faith and say, "If the Lord's will, I will do this or that."

It may be that getting to point B may be disastrous for you. That's why we must get our directions from the One that is head of our lives and use His wisdom for our guide, each and every day of our lives.

We don't know for sure what our next steps will be. We can only assume that we will accomplish what we start out to do.

To get to our next destination will require planning, praying and using wisdom to wait on God for answers.

His way can also mean that we must go another way, because there is danger in the path we have taken.

In this life, one thing we know for sure is that we are going to die one day. The other thing we can know is that if we truly accept Jesus Christ as our Lord and Savior, we will see God in peace.

What Are Your Plans for Today?

Planning is always in order. It should be the order of each day.

To plan today means that you are organized and you will be ahead of the game of life that is before you.

Our plans for today should be carefully sought out. We should make sure our plans line up with reality. The things we do today should be in total harmony with what is right and honest.

What we plan will determine our success or failure in our life's struggles.

Things we plan for will not always come out like we want them to.

Sometimes, we will have to make an adjustment to our plans because of some unseen problem that will pop up in the way.

Our plans for today will work if we are moving in the right direction toward our goal that we have set.

In order to be successful in our plans, we must see if our plans are acceptable to God's plans for our lives.

We must incorporate prayer into our plans for our plans to work. We must make sure our plans are the plans God will be pleased with.

The Mirror

What do you see when you look in the mirror?

Do you like what you see, or maybe dislike this or that about yourself? The answer is, you are what you are.

Perhaps you may be looking on the outside of you, which is less important than you think.

The real you is locked up inside of you and is manifested by what comes out of your heart, that you stored each and every day.

It comes by way of your words you speak, the actions you take, the things you do, good or not so good.

When I look in my mirror, I want to see a person that is honest in heart and soul, looking unto God for strength and courage to be all that will make me a person that God can count on to be a reflection of what authentic love is.

And I hope looking into the mirror will show me a person that is focused, that is looking ahead by preparing for what the future will afford me.

Attention

The central point of attention is the key point of focus. Learning is getting prepared for the future.

Success comes because of attention.

Attention causes one to stay in focus of what is being said.

Attention will help us do things better. Attention takes concentration, to think about processing words that will bring positive actions that would make things happen to benefit society.

We should remember as much as we can, time is very serious, it waits on no one, it is moving each day and hour, going about its business. We should be aware of how time is passing away, making history as the days go by.

What we learn today will shape our tomorrows.

There is no way we can go wrong, if we pay attention and work each day to attain the skills and knowledge that will help us prepare for what lies before us. That will help us master our lives, the method of paying attention to what we hear, see, and experience.

Generosity

I have found out that life on this earth is not complete unless we give and share with others what we have been blessed with.

We are tested with plenty of resources to see if we can give to someone that is in need.

Just think about it, how much has God charged you and me for the air we breathe each day? How much does he charge us for the water we go down to the spring and drink? How much does he ask for us to rent His earth? Something to think about, isn't it?

Giving is a trait of God, for it is more blessed to give than to receive.

Gratitude exalts a person to a higher level and his return will always be much more than he gives out.

We are on this earth to be a blessing to someone.

What if every able person just gave something to some needy person? I wonder what the results would be.

We are blessed to live in a generous country.

Success

How to achieve success in life? Build on a solid foundation. Start with the principles of God's Word and build upward on the contents from the read Word. They are true and faithful, without any doubt.

Then pray every day and meditate on the words you have read from the scriptures. Then follow everything that is right and true in life. Don't let it slip away from you, not for one moment.

You will be tried and tested to the very top of your ability, to see how much you believe what you have read. And the world will be watching you daily. So, it is very important to believe what you get from the Holy Scriptures and watch always. The scriptures must be fulfilled and the things you have read will all come to pass one day, sooner or later; God never lies.

Those getting grounded and settled are persons who love God with all their hearts. For only iron sharpens iron, and who you associate with will be just like you each day. Let God always be honored in all you do and say. Don't forget to apologize if necessary and always seek to better your relationship with your fellowman. Never do evil for evil.

Live above reproach and always do your best in all you attempt.

God will bless you. Stay in the race; a lot of times we may fail, but never quit.

Concluding Words

My prayer for you:
may God's grace, mercy, and love keep you each day.

Amen

About the Author

Miller Allen was born in 1939. While his early life was filled with challenges such as poverty and alcohol abuse in his family, he was determined to break the mold and become successful. In 1958, he accepted Jesus Christ into his life. The writings in this book reveal lessons learned through his many experiences. He is married to the former Alice Powell. They have been blessed with two children, eight grandchildren, and twelve greatgrandchildren.

Milton Keynes UK
Ingram Content Group UK Ltd.
UKHW022228051124
450708UK00014B/1000